Erika Cornstuble Koff believes having a good day depends entirely on how good her hair looks. She is a writer and comedian who lives in Los Angeles with her husband, Ben, who makes all of her days better.

Paul Seaburn hopes this book brings you lots of nice days, or at least a few laugh-filled ones. He's a comedy writer, author, and teacher whose television credits include *Taylor's Attic*, *The Tonight Show*, and *Politically Incorrect*. He is the author of *Jestercises & Gamestorms* and teaches "Creative Thinking Through Comedy," a program for gifted students. Paul lives in Spring, Texas, with his wife, Donna.

Louis Weber, CEO
Publications International, Ltd.
7373 North Cicero Avenue
Lincolnwood, Illinois 60712

Permission is never granted for commercial purposes.

ISBN-13: 978-1-4127-1480-8
ISBN-10: 1-4127-1480-X

Manufactured in China.

8 7 6 5 4 3 2 1

HAVE A NICE DAY!

pil

Publications International, Ltd.

Laughter cures all

of life's bumps and bruises.

Hold hands with **your future.**

Nothing makes it

"ALL BETTER" like a

HUG FROM GRANDMA.

If you learn to MULTITASK,

there's ALWAYS time to PLAY.

E very Wednesday afternoon, Spike **BABYSAT** the kids until Mrs. McInerny got back from the BEAUTY SHOP.

It's easier to

SUCCEED when

EVERYONE'S PULLING

for you.

"*W*hatever IT is,

NEITHER of us did IT."

Small pleasures can help to
"POP" the everyday monotony.

Make a DATE with your INNER CHILD.

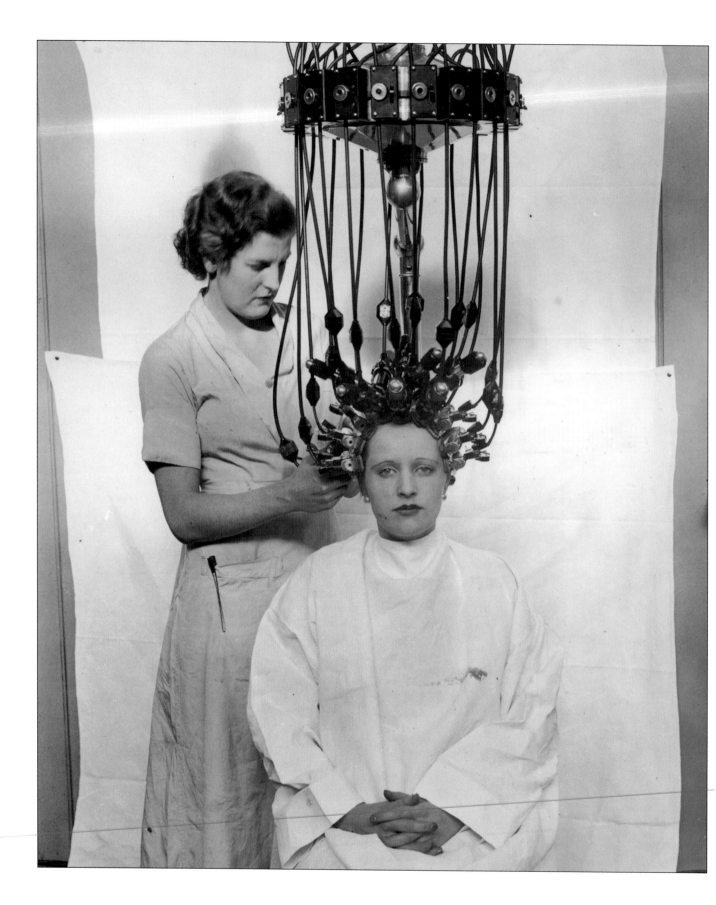

With the new Electro-curler, you can KISS both your BAD HAIR DAYS *and* your SHORT-TERM MEMORY GOOD-BYE!

Sometimes life HANGS you out TO DRY.

Always **SEPARATE**

yourself from

the FLOCK.

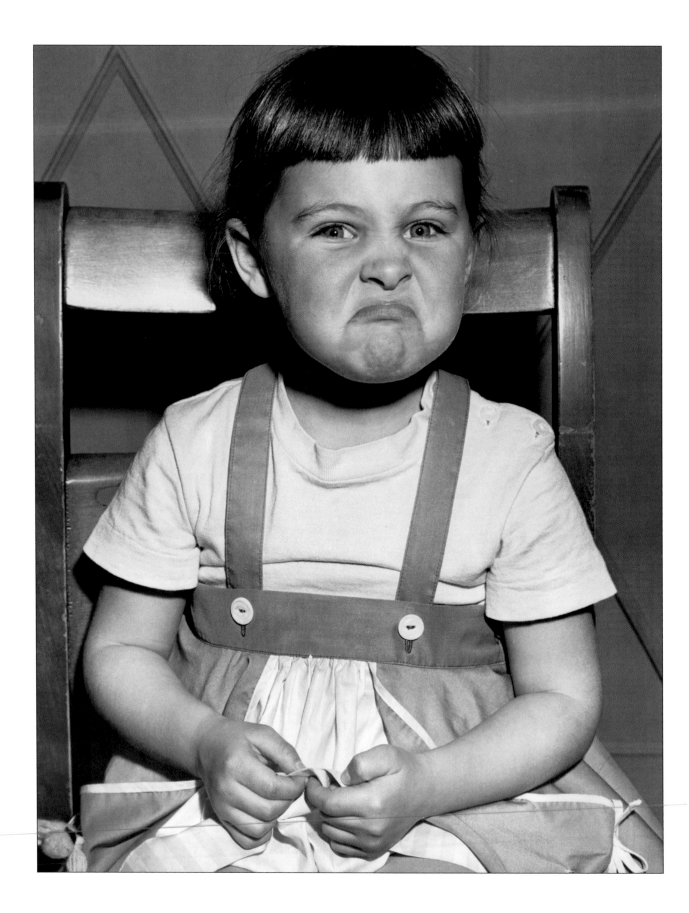

Everyone needs a

TIME-OUT

OCCASIONALLY.

Doing the
Cancun CANCAN!

Don't let OBSTACLES

squash your ENTHUSIASM.

Ice cream makes a **SMILE** sweeter.

SURPRISE someone you love with a

SHOWER OF AFFECTION.

Never settle for

the GARDEN-VARIETY.

You're **NEVER TOO YOUNG**

to learn how to

PARALLEL PARK.

It's a BIG WORLD out there.

Bring **CHAPERONES**.

Say it with a CARD.

Say it with FLOWERS.

BUT SAY IT.

The **FIRST DAY** of anything can be a LITTLE STRESSFUL.

You never outgrow RECESS.

Sometimes you're

SANDWICHED BETWEEN

your dreams and reality.

Sometimes you're

SANDWICHED BETWEEN

sandwiches.

And sometimes you're

THE SANDWICH.

"Oh, say can you see, by the dawn's early light…" GRANDMA LISTENED through THREE VERSES and never once thought about the PHONE BILL.

Sun. Surf. Sand.

SENSATIONAL.

When your life

becomes a **ROLLER COASTER**,

get your best friend

and sit in the **FRONT SEAT.**

"One for ME,

one for YOU."

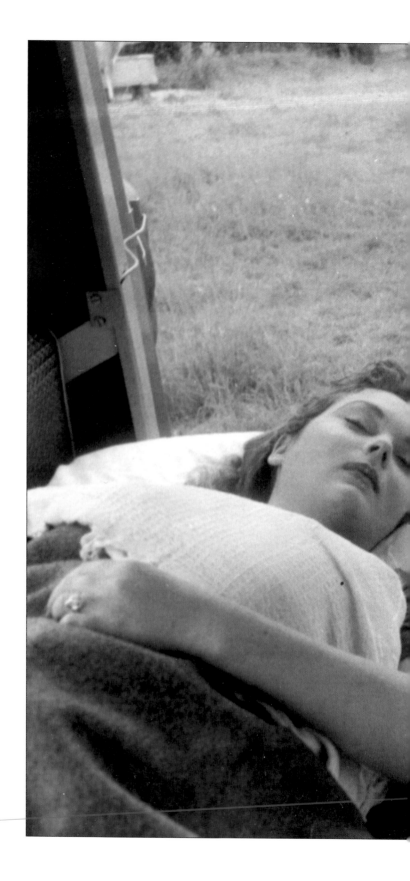

Some days you need to **PARTY** 'til the cows come **HOME.**

B REAKFAST is

the **MOST IMPORTANT**

meal of the DAY.

TURNABOUT

IS **FAIR PLAY**!

Your TALENT may be unusual,

but *always* MAKE THE MOST of it.

You know it's a

ROUGH DAY when even

your TOYS TURN against you.

My merry Ch... DOLLY'S FACIAL KIT SAFE AND HARMLESS

JUST LIKE MOMMY'S! My merry MAKE-UP SAFE AND HARMLESS

How do you get to be an AVON LADY?

PRACTICE, **PRACTICE,** PRACTICE.

"My husband THINKS

I'm at BRIDGE CLUB."

LIFE IS SHORT.

When in doubt, **DRINK CHOCOLATE.**

EVERY BABY should

get this kind of **ATTENTION.**

Sometimes a **COFFEE BREAK** makes everything **WORTHWHILE.**

One tiny LAUGH,

a WORLD of JOY.

When **LIFE** gives
you a TRAFFIC JAM,
have a **PICNIC.**

Beneath every **TOUGH-GUY** exterior,

there's a LITTLE BOY crying for ATTENTION.

A SMILE and a good sense of HUMOR can get you through even the most EMBARRASSING situations.

If you start the day CRABBY, you'll

end the day CRABBY.

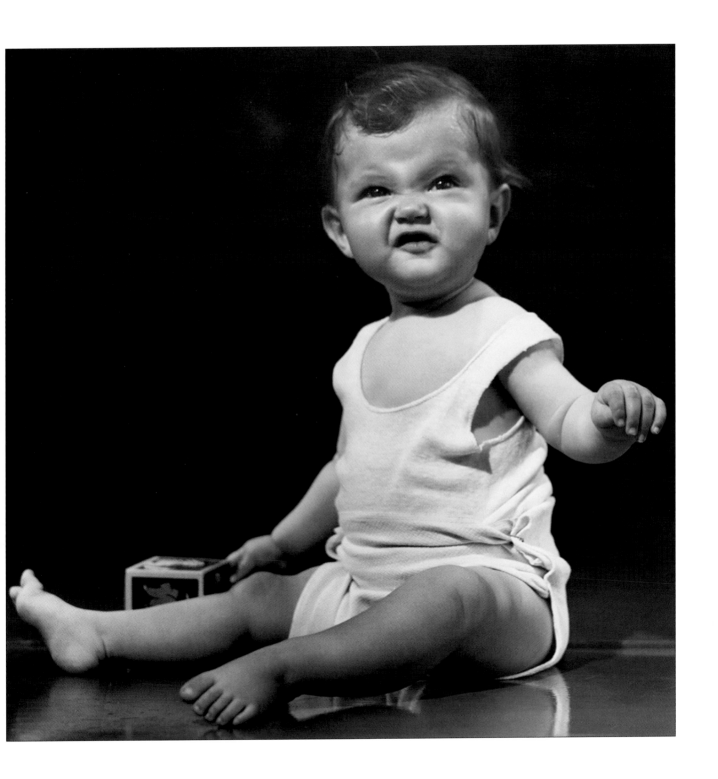

A quick **FLIGHT** back to **CHILDHOOD.**

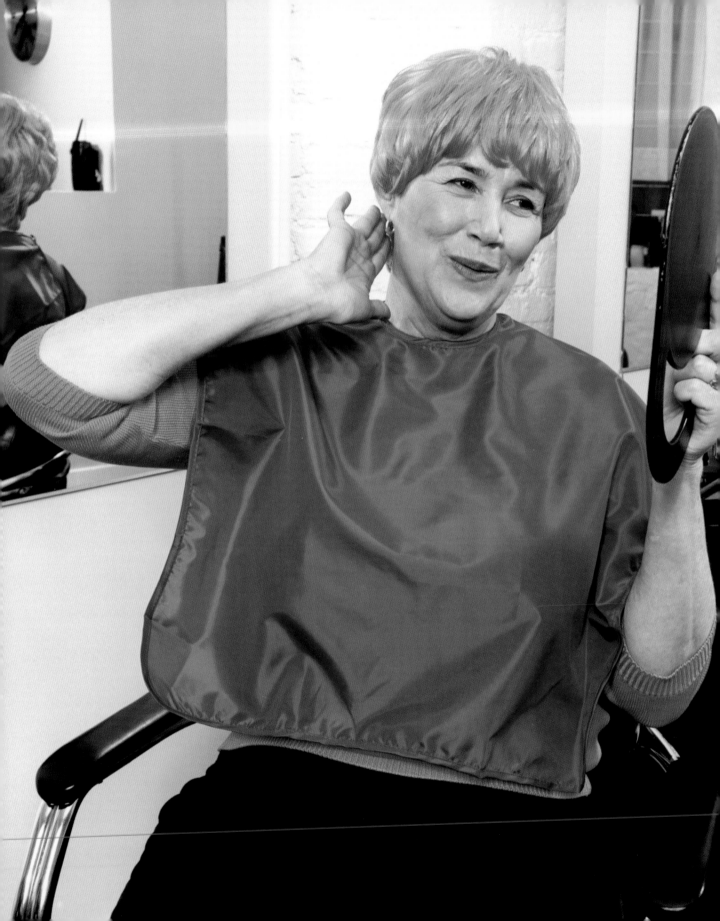

If you're feeling BLUE,

you just need to think PINK.

Sometimes the difference between a GOOD day and a GREAT day is one more SCOOP.